Stan Lee

Stan Lee

COMIC BOOK GENIUS

STEVEN OTFINOSKI

FRANKLIN WATTS
A Division of Scholastic Inc.
New York Toronto London Auckland Sydney
Mexico City New Delhi Hong Kong
Danbury, Connecticut

All Photographs © 2007: AP/Wide World Photos: 28; Corbis Images: 35, 36, 38, 40, 42, 44, 48, 50, 53, 54, 56, 62, 65 (© 2005 Marvel), 9, 18 (Bettmann), 13 (Marjory Collins), 70 (Owen Franken), covers (Kim Kulish), 69 (Marc Lecureuil), 80 (Charles O'Rear), 75 (Neal Preston), 76 (Ted Streshinsky); Everett Collection, Inc.: 88, 94 (Columbia Pictures), 60, 72; Getty Images: 96 (Vince Bucci), 11 (FPG/Hulton Archive), 78 (Rob Kinmonth/Time & Life Pictures), 22 (Ruth Orkin/Hulton Archive), 83 (Allan Tannenbaum/Time & Life Pictures); Photofest: 74 (CBS), 93 (Zade Rosenthal/Columbia Pictures), 84 (Jim Sheldon/New World Pictures), 2; Stan Lee: 6, 14, 20, 25, 26, 58, 67; Superstock, Inc./Dynamic Graphics Value: 32; The Kirby Estate and the Jack Kirby Collector magazine, www.twomorrows.com: 30; WireImage.com/Albert L. Ortega: 86.

Library of Congress Cataloging-in-Publication Data
Otfinoski, Steven.
  Stan Lee : comic book genius / by Steven Otfinoski.
     p. cm. — (Great life stories)
  Includes bibliographical references and index.
  ISBN-10: 0-531-13873-9
  ISBN-13: 978-0-531-13873-1
  1. Lee, Stan. 2. Cartoonists—United States—Biography. I. Title. II. Series.
  PN6727.L39Z83 2006
  791.5092—dc22   2005030646

1 2 3 4 5 6 7 8 9 10 R 16 15 14 13 12 11 10 09 08 07

Contents

Stanley (left) was Jack and Celia's first son. Their second, Larry, was born during the Great Depression.

ONE

A Child of the Depression

The man who molded the modern comic book and raised it to the level of an art form was born on December 28, 1922, in an apartment on 98th Street and West End Avenue in New York City. It was a city that, decades later, he would make the home of many of his superheroes. Stanley Martin Lieber was born to Jack and Celia Lieber, who had immigrated to the United States from Romania in Eastern Europe. Stanley's father was a dress cutter in Manhattan's garment district, and his mother was a housewife. His brother, Larry, his only sibling, was nine years his junior.

HARD TIMES FOR THE LIEBERS

By the time of Larry's birth, the nation was in the throes of the Great Depression (1929–1941), the most devastating economic period in American history. Millions of Americans had lost their jobs and were out of work. Jack Lieber was among them. He tried opening his own business, a diner, with his savings, but it failed. The family moved from West End Avenue to a cheaper, smaller apartment uptown in Washington Heights. The lack of money drove Jack and Celia to quarrel constantly.

"I realized at an early age how the specter of poverty, the never-ending worry about not having enough money to buy groceries or to pay the rent, can cast a cloud over a marriage," Stan wrote many years later.

In this new neighborhood, Stan attended DeWitt Clinton High School. A good student, he was younger than his classmates and something of an outsider. With few friends, he turned to movies and reading for solace. He devoured mysteries such as the Hardy Boys Mystery Series and the Sherlock Holmes stories of Arthur Conan Doyle. He also loved the science-fiction novels of H. G. Wells and the Tarzan adventure stories of Edgar Rice Burroughs. As he grew older, he discovered the plays of William Shakespeare and developed a love for the theater and acting.

To help the family finances, young Stan got a job as an usher at the Rivoli movie theater on Broadway. It was the perfect job for a dreamy boy who was enthralled by the magic of the movies. In the swashbuckling films of Errol Flynn, his favorite actor, he could escape from life's grim realities.

A BUDDING WRITER

Like many avid young readers, Stan soon tried his hand at writing. He made up his own illustrated stories, creating his first comic books. When he was fifteen, he entered a student writing contest sponsored by the *New York-Herald Tribune* newspaper. Contestants were to write about what they considered to be the biggest news story of the week in an essay of five hundred words or less. Stan's first essay was given an award, and an editor at the *Tribune* suggested that he consider writing as a career. Stan liked that

Stan grew up during the Great Depression, when millions were out of work and lined up for food and jobs.

idea. Still in high school, he took a part-time job writing obituaries, or death notices, for a news service. He also tried his hand at writing publicity for the National Tuberculosis Hospital in Denver, Colorado.

These experiences helped develop his writing skills, but he wasn't attracted to either journalism or publicity as a full-time career. After graduating high school, he joined the Federal Theatre Project (FTP), which was established under the Depression-era Works Progress Administration (WPA). He joined to pursue acting—and to pursue a young girl he liked who also belonged to the FTP. That romance went nowhere, and Stan left the theater job. He realized he needed a steady, full-time job to support himself and help his struggling family. A family connection led him to just such a job.

TIMELY COMICS

Stan's older cousin Jean was married to Martin Goodman, the owner and publisher of Timely Comics, a comic book company located in the McGraw-Hill Building on 42nd Street and Ninth Avenue. Stan's uncle Robbie Solomon also worked for Goodman. In 1940, Stan landed the position of "good all-round gofer" at Timely at the starting salary of $8 a week.

Goodman had begun his publishing career some years earlier as a creator of pulp fiction magazines. These inexpensive paperback collections of crime and suspense stories were extremely popular in the 1920s and 1930s. By the late 1930s, however, comic books, a new medium, were quickly outselling pulps, and Goodman decided to switch to comics.

In October 1939, Timely put out the first issue of *Marvel Mystery*

Comics. To compete with Superman, the leading superhero at National Comics (a competitor that later became DC Comics), Timely created its own superheroes: the Human Torch and the Sub-Mariner. Sub-Mariner was one of the first anti-heroes (evil superheroes) in comic books. After the destruction of his home—the undersea continent of Atlantis—by the people of the surface world, he sought revenge on them. Sub-Mariner and the Human Torch were later joined by Captain America, created by freelance artist Jack Kirby and writer Joe Simon. Captain America, who debuted in March 1941, was a patriotic superhero who fought the German Nazis, invaders of Western and Eastern Europe during World War II (1939–1945).

Stan got his first opportunity to write for Timely in the third issue of *Captain America.* To qualify for inexpensive magazine postal rates, comic books had to include some straight,

Manhattan was the base for the major comic book publishers during the Golden Age.

non-illustrated text in their pages. Stan was assigned to write a two-page story he called "Captain America Foils the Traitor's Revenge." A few issues later, he wrote his first script for an actual comic. It was a filler piece titled "Headline Hunter, Foreign Correspondent."

When faced with having to sign his name to the story, Stan decided to cut his first name in half and change the y in "Stanley" to a second e, becoming "Stan Lee." His main reason for choosing a pen name was, he

Early Comic Books

The first comic book to be sold on newsstands was the monthly *Famous Funnies*, published in 1934 by the Eastern Color Printing Company. It was the brainstorm of salesman Max Gaines, whose son William would one day create *MAD* magazine. *Famous Funnies* wasn't what we think of as a comic book today. It was merely bound collections of the popular weekly Sunday color comic strips that were published in American newspapers.

The following year, National Comics put out *New Fun Comics*, the first comic book to include original stories not first published in the Sunday funnies. These early comic books lived up to their name. Most of the strips were humorous gag comics with little story line. That changed in 1937, when National released the first issue of *Detective Comics*, which included stories of adventure and mystery.

The next year, *National's Action Comics* introduced the first superhero, Superman, created by writer Jerry Siegel and artist Joe Shuster, neither of whom was much older than Stan Lieber. With Superman, comic books became the reading matter of choice for millions of American children, especially boys. The age of the superhero had begun, and the comic book entered its Golden Age.

later explained, "because I felt someday I'd be writing the Great American Novel and I didn't want to use my real name on these silly little comics." Little did he know at the time that he would be spending the rest of his working life creating "these silly little comics."

The popularity of Superman, the first superhero, spawned the creation of hundreds of superheroes.

Stan Lee's first steady full-time job led to his lifelong career writing comic books.

Love and War

Martin Goodman ran Timely Comics with a skilled hand and a tight fist. As was the custom in the comics industry, writers and artists worked on a strictly freelance basis and were paid by the page with no regular salary. They also received no royalties on anything they wrote or drew. Artist Jack Kirby and writer Joe Simon were the only full-time employees, other than Stan, who received regular salaries. They also shared in the profits of the characters they created for Timely—the most important of them being Captain America.

One day in early 1941, Kirby and Simon learned from the company accountant that Goodman had been cheating them out of profits for Captain America. They both promptly quit and went over to the competition, National Comics, where they were each offered a salary of $500 a week.

Jack Kirby—
Comic Artist Extraordinaire

One of comic books' greatest artists was born Jacob Kurtzburg in New York City in 1917. He began his career as an artist working as an "in-betweener" at the Fleischer Studios in New York, doing the fill-in animation on cartoons featuring Popeye and Betty Boop. Animation wasn't Kirby's thing, though, and he left Fleischer in 1937 to draw comic strips for a small news syndicate. Some of his creations include such forgotten strips as Black Buccaneer and Socko the Seadog.

In 1940, Kirby teamed up with writer Joe Simon at Timely to create Captain America. Their collaboration lasted sixteen years. In 1958, Kirby returned to Timely, by then renamed Atlas Comics, and became a key player in the rebirth of the patriotic superhero. With Lee, he co-created the Fantastic Four, the Incredible Hulk, the X-Men, Thor, the Silver Surfer, and many other memorable superheroes.

Kirby was more than just an excellent comic artist. He had the dramatic instincts of a playwright and the sophisticated eye of a filmmaker. "In virtually every one of his panels there was something to marvel at," wrote Stan Lee. "As amazing as his artwork was, he also depicted a story so clearly that you could almost follow it without reading the words."

After years of fruitful collaboration, Kirby had a falling-out with Lee and Marvel Comics over money and rights, and he left Marvel in 1970. He continued to draw and create new comics for other publishers and reunited with Lee on other projects until his retirement in 1987. Jack Kirby died of heart failure on February 6, 1994, leaving behind a body of work that is unsurpassed in the history of comic book art.

STAN IN CHARGE

Goodman decided to promote Stan to editorial and art director until he could find someone more experienced for the position. Not quite nineteen, Stan felt a little out of his depth in the job, but he did his best. As time went on, Goodman was pleased with the work his wife's cousin was doing and decided that anyone more experienced would only ask for more money.

Timely cranked out comic books like sausages, and Stan quickly found himself writing most of the comics himself. To avoid making Timely look like a one-man operation, he created a number of new humorous pen names, including Stan Martin, Stan Leen, S. T. Anley, and Neel Nats (Stan Leen backward).

Unlike National Comics and a few other bolder competitors, Timely never set the trends; it only followed them, according to Stan. Caring little for creativity and everything for profits, Martin Goodman was happy to follow the crowd and get his share of the market. He never strived to make his comics better than anyone else's. It was a philosophy that would later drive Stan to distraction. But at the time, Stan was content and happy to be working and making a decent living.

STAN GOES TO WAR

On December 7, 1941, the Japanese bombed the U.S. naval base at Pearl Harbor, Hawaii, home to America's Pacific Fleet, in a sneak attack. Numerous ships were destroyed, and hundreds of men were killed. The following day, the United States declared war on Japan and its allies,

Germany and Italy. The United States had entered World War II. Captain America was put to work in his comic book fighting the Nazis and Japanese, and Stan Lee was ready to do his part in the war. He enlisted in the U.S. Army in November 1942 and was sent to Fort Monmouth in New Jersey for basic training. Placed in the signal corps, Stan expected to be sent overseas to work in communications. Instead, to his great dis-

Hollywood filmmaker Frank Capra (right) wrote manuals and scripts for the military with Stan Lee while serving in the Army during World War II.

appointment, he was sent to Astoria in Queens, New York, to become part of the signal corps' training-film division.

Stan had been identified as a professional writer and found himself put into the category of "playwright" by the Army. Within this select group of nine men, Stan was definitely the low man on the totem pole. The other "playwrights" included Hollywood filmmaker Frank Capra, *New Yorker* magazine cartoonist Charles Addams, and novelist and playwright (the only actual playwright in the group) William Saroyan.

Stan and the others wrote scripts for military training films and instructional manuals. The work wasn't terribly demanding, and Stan found time at night and on weekends to write comic book scripts for Timely and mail them back to Manhattan. After three years in the Army, he returned to civilian life in 1945, when the war ended.

BACK TO WORK

Now twenty-three, Stan moved into New York's Almanac Hotel. Every morning, he walked forty blocks south to the Timely offices, which were located in the Empire State Building. The workload for Timely's editorial director was incredibly demanding. With the war over, the wartime paper shortage ended and more comics were printed than ever before.

Under Martin Goodman's controlling hand, Timely remained as timely as ever, but it was no more innovative than in past years. Stan tried to bring some freshness to the comics, however modestly. He had the idea of creating a team of superheroes called The All Winner Squad. The fearless quintet was composed of Captain America, the Human Torch, Sub-Mariner, the Whizzer (a fast-moving superhero), and Miss

Some of the characters Stan created while at Timely weren't commercial successes, but several became the models for his most successful superheroes.

America (a feeble attempt to attract more female readers). The All Winner Squad was a loser in sales, and the series was discontinued after only two issues. But Stan had created a blueprint for a team of supcrheroes that would prove extremely successful in years to come.

Superheroes in general were losing their appeal with comic book readers, who were looking for more real-life heroes in the postwar era. Crime fighters and cops were beginning to replace superheroes as comic book favorites. By the early 1950s, the Human Torch, Sub-Mariner, and even Captain America would all be retired. As the superheroes departed, so did much of the imagination and creativity that writers and artists poured into their adventures. The Golden Age of Comic Books seemed to be drawing to a close.

ROMANCE AND MARRIAGE

Stan was enjoying his off-hours from Timely. He was a carefree bachelor, and New York was full of pretty girls. He took his dates on romantic horse rides in Central Park and boat rides on Central Park Lake. But he hadn't found the girl he wanted to settle down with. In 1947, a cousin told him about a model he knew named Betty, and he thought Stan might like to take her out. Stan went to the model's agency and was met at the door by another model, a gorgeous redhead with a British accent who took his breath away. Her name was Joan Clayton Boocock. Soon the two were dating. Stan was in love, but there was one problem. Joan was married. She was, however, separated from her husband and about to fly to Reno, Nevada, for a divorce.

Afraid she'd meet someone new in Reno and forget about him, Stan decided to follow Joanie, as he called her, to Nevada. When he arrived, he discovered his fears were well grounded. Joanie was being romanced by a rich Western oilman who bore a resemblance to John Wayne. But Stan's ardor and East Coast charm won out. He and Joanie were married on December 5, 1947, in the same building where her divorce had been finalized. The sixty-second ceremony resulted in a marriage that to date has lasted close to sixty years.

The happy couple caught a train for New York City. They took no honeymoon, settling immediately into a brownstone on 96th Street on the East Side. Then it was back to writing comic books for Stan Lee.

Competing comic book publishers were constantly vying for the attention of young readers.

THREE

In a Rut

As the superheroes of the Golden Age declined in popularity, new genres took over in the comic book industry. Besides crime stories, many other comics became the rage in the late 1940s—Westerns, romance stories, teen humor, and funny animal comics. As usual, Martin Goodman followed these trends with such titles as *Official True Crime Cases, Amazing Detective Cases, Wild Western Comics, Two-Gun Kid, Romance Tales, Millie the Model,* and *Ziggy Pig and Silly Seal.*

The start of the Korean War in 1950 brought a new comic book genre to the fore—war comics. Entertaining Comics (EC) came out with *Frontline Combat* and *Two-Fisted Tales,* two wartime titles written and drawn by the gifted Harvey Kurtzman. Timely fell in line with its own *War Comics, Combat Kelly,* and other titles. Weary of following trends instead of

EC Comics—
First Name in Horror

EC Comics, founded by comic pioneer Max Gaines in 1945, began life as Educational Comics, retelling stories from history, science, and the Bible in cartoon format. When Gaines died in a boating accident in 1947, his son William took over the company. Bill Gaines dropped the educational comics and made the E in EC stand for "Entertaining."

At first, EC put out Westerns and romances just as other comic publishers did. Then in 1950, Gaines and his top artist, Al Feldstein, decided to try something new. Inspired by the suspense and horror radio programs they had enjoyed in their youth, they put out a series of gruesome, tongue-in-cheek horror comics. *The Vault of Horror* and *The Crypt of Terror* (later renamed *Tales from the Crypt*) were followed by two equally imaginative sci-fi comics, *Weird Science* and *Weird Fantasy*. These comic books featured some of the best art and writing in the business, and they were among the most popular with readers.

When a wave of censorship swept the comic industry in the mid-1950s, EC was hit the hardest. Gaines soon abandoned all his comic titles and concentrated on a satirical comic book developed in 1952 by artist-writer Harvey Kurtzman. To avoid the censorship of the Comics Code Authority, Gaines turned the comic called *Tales Calculated to Drive You Mad* into *MAD* magazine in the summer of 1955. More than fifty years later, *MAD* magazine is still one of the best-known humor magazines in America.

making them, Stan Lee confessed in his autobiography that "I sometimes felt we should change the name of our company to In a Rut Comics."

MARRIED LIFE

Stan found comfort and reassurance in his home life away from the office. When his mother died, he and Joanie took in his fifteen-year-old brother, Larry. Stan and Larry had not been close as children, due to the nine-year difference in their ages. But now a common interest in comics would draw them closer together, and Larry would later become one of his brother's collaborators. The family of three moved from Manhattan to a small house in Woodmere, Long Island. Here, in 1950, Joanie gave birth to their first child, Joan Celia. Stan called her Little Joan to distinguish her from her mother.

Stan Lee and his wife, Joanie, have been married for nearly sixty years.

Tragedy would enter their lives in 1953, when Joanie gave birth to a second daughter, Jan. The infant died three days after she was born, and doctors told Joanie she could not have any more children. The couple

Little Joan (above) was only about three when the Lees' other daughter died.

looked into adoption but didn't pursue it. In a rare somber moment in his autobiography, Stan wrote, "Looking back, I'm not sure we made the right decision, but life goes on."

COMICS UNDER ATTACK

The year 1954 was a turning point for the comic book industry. Dr. Fredric Wertham, a psychiatrist, published his book *Seduction of the Innocent*. It blamed comic books for everything bad in American society, from juvenile delinquency to encroaching communism. Horror and crime comics, with their exaggerated violence and suggestive sexual content, took the brunt of Wertham's attack, but he also went after superheroes. He pointed to "fantasies of sadistic joy in seeing other people punished" while the hero remained immune, labeling this the Superman Complex. He even went so far as to claim that superheroes and their teen sidekicks, such as Batman and Robin, were bound in homosexual relationships!

At this time, suspicions about communism and other threats to the American way of life were running high. Congress held hearings to determine whether people were engaged in activities that would erode American society. Entertainers, publishers, and many other people were called before investigative committees. That included Bill Gaines and Stan Lee, who vigorously defended their comic books. Lee even debated Dr. Wertham on a number of occasions and usually won the debate. In one of their debates, Wertham claimed that a survey he conducted showed that most kids in reform school read comic books. "If you do another survey," retorted Lee, "you'll find that most of the kids who

In the mid-1950s, comic books were blamed for causing delinquency and violence. Some organizations collected the comics to burn them.

drink milk are comic book readers. Should we ban milk?"

The connection Wertham made between comics and violent behavior in young people was a shaky one at best. In fact, his theories have been thoroughly discredited by psychologists and other experts in the field. But in this era of increasing fear and overriding conformity, Wertham's attacks were taken seriously. The entire comic book industry was in danger. To limit the damage, the comic publishers formed the Comic Magazine Association of America (CMAA). This group established the Comics Code Authority (CCA) to regulate the content of comic books.

FROM TIMELY TO ATLAS

During this period, Timely Comics changed its name to Atlas Comics, after the Greek god who carried the universe on his shoulders. While the company was no world-bearing

The Comics Code Authority

The Comics Code Authority (CCA), a self-censoring group, was established in 1954. Under the code, every comic book published in America had to be sent to the CCA office, where members would closely examine its content. They would suggest ways to make stories acceptable. If the publisher refused to make the changes, the comic would not receive the CCA's seal of approval on its cover. Without this seal, many distributors would not accept that issue for sale. Almost overnight, sexual content and much of the violence in comics disappeared. Unfortunately, so did most of the imagination and creativity. By being careful not to offend anyone, comic books became predictable, uninspired, and bland.

giant, it emerged from the events of 1954 in better shape than many comic book companies. Atlas's titles were less controversial than those of other companies such as EC, which soon got out of the comic book business entirely. Goodman retired the few superheroes left in his stable and put out inoffensive titles that featured more funny animals, comic teenagers, and the old, reliable Western outlaws and lawmen.

But the chilling effect on the industry continued into the late 1950s. As sales fell off, Atlas was forced to tighten its budget. Goodman ordered Stan to fire the entire staff, something Stan hated to do. Goodman also closed his distribution operations and hired a private distributor. The new distributor went bankrupt two weeks later, and Atlas was without a distributor for its comics. Goodman was forced to approach his rival National Comics (now called DC) for help with distribution. DC agreed to help, but it would only carry a dozen of Atlas's titles. Overnight, Atlas went from producing nearly eighty comic book

Jack Kirby co-created some of the most memorable comic book characters including Captain America, the Incredible Hulk, and the X-Men.

titles to a mere twelve. It would take several years for Atlas to regain its independence and its extensive lineup of titles.

THE RETURN OF JACK KIRBY

One bright spot on the horizon was the return of artist Jack Kirby to Atlas in 1958. Another gifted artist, Steve Ditko, had come on board in 1956. Together with Stan, Kirby and Ditko created several science-fiction titles that had more imagination than all the company's other comics put together. Their exciting stories with outlandish monsters just managed to skirt around the Comics Code by employing little fatal violence and gore. "While DC used sci-fi to exalt the virtue of scientific progress and the certainty of peace through technology, Marvel [Atlas] spoke to the anxieties of the atomic age," wrote Bradford Wright in his book *Comic Book Nation*.

Despite the success of Atlas's science-fiction comics, sales hit an all-time low by 1960. And so did Stan Lee. He had spent more than half his life writing and publishing comic books. Now, nearing the age of forty, he was completely burnt out. Stan was ready to call it quits with comic books and try something new.

Comic books were an especially popular form of entertainment for children growing up in the 1950s and 1960s.

FOUR

Fantastic Developments

An exciting new era began for Stan Lee in 1961, and its inspiration came from an unexpected source—his unadventurous publisher, Martin Goodman. Goodman had a golf date with Jack Liebowitz, the publisher at DC Comics. Liebowitz told Goodman that DC's newest title, *The Justice League of America*, was selling briskly. The Justice League was made up of many of DC's most popular superheroes. Goodman, spotting a new trend, went back to the office and told Stan to put together a team of superheroes. The idea wasn't entirely original: Stan had tried a similar team years earlier, but it had failed to sell. Goodman suggested that Stan try bringing together three Timely

The Justice League of America

A year before Stan Lee created his new line of superheroes, DC Comics had already begun its own revival of superheroes with the Justice League of America (JLA). To create it, DC editor Julius Schwartz revived an older organization of superheroes from the 1940s—the Justice Society of America—changing the original name to make it sound less stodgy.

The Justice League's original lineup had seven members. The big names were Superman, Batman, and Wonder Woman. The second-tier heroes were Aquaman, the Flash, Green Lantern, and an adventurer known as the Martian Manhunter. As the series' popularity grew, more and more superheroes were recruited into the league, including exotic DC characters such as the Black Canary, the Red Tornado, and the Phantom Stranger.

Not one to quit on a good thing, Schwartz revived the old Justice Society in 1963 to join forces with the Justice League. The two groups would have an annual reunion to fight evildoers.

After twenty-five years of success, JLA's readership fell off in the 1980s. To revive interest, DC dumped all the traditional heroes and introduced a new roster of contemporary, ethnically diverse characters for a kind of United Nations of superheroes. The idea proved to be a dud, and DC disbanded the league in 1987. The JLA has been revived several times since then with the classic lineup, but it never recaptured the spirit of the original comic book.

heroes from the 1940s—Captain America, Sub-Mariner, and the Human Torch.

Stan wasn't keen on the idea at first. He still had his mind set on leaving Atlas and trying something new. But Joanie talked him into giving the comics one more shot. She urged him to do something fresh and original, exactly the way he wanted to. If Goodman and the readers didn't like his new creation, fine—he was out the door. He had nothing to lose by giving it his best.

Stan went to work, ignoring Goodman's advice, and created a quartet of brand-new superheroes, unlike any of the past—the Fantastic Four. "They were the kind of team I had been longing to write about," Stan later wrote. "Heroes who were less than perfect. Heroes who didn't always get along with each other, but heroes who could be counted on when the chips were down."

With both human flaws and superpowers, the Fantastic Four were the first superheroes of their kind.

THE FANTASTIC FOUR

The first issue of *The Fantastic Four*, written by Stan Lee and drawn by Jack Kirby, was dated November 1961. From the get-go, these characters were something new to the world of superheroes. The basic story line went like this. Scientist Reed Richards had created a super spaceship that he hoped would beat the Soviet Union in the race for space. But

Comic book readers immediately related to the Fantastic Four, and the first issue sold out.

the U.S. government, which funded the project, had doubts about the ship's safety and put it on hold. Reed, who believed in his ship, wouldn't wait. His pilot and friend, Ben Grimm; his girlfriend, Sue Storm; her teenage brother, Johnny; and Reed stole inside the spaceship one day and blasted off.

Reed's overconfidence almost got them all killed. The spaceship passed through a shower of cosmic rays before crashing back to Earth. The unearthly rays altered each of the four in different ways. Reed developed the ability to change his body into any shape he chose and became Mr. Fantastic. Sue gained the ability to make herself invisible and became the Invisible Girl. Johnny was able to fly through the air and burst into flames. He became the Human Torch. (Other than his name and superpower, the new Human Torch had little else in common with Timely Comics' earlier Human Torch. That character had been an android, an artificial man created by a scientist.) Ben's transformation was the most amazing of all. He turned into a monstrous creature with scaly orange skin called the Thing. He was the only one of the four who could not transform back into his original self.

The four friends quickly decided to use their new abilities to battle evil and further the good of humankind. But that's where the similarities to the Justice League of America ended. As Reed said in one of their early adventures: "What's the matter with the four of us? Whenever we're not fighting some menace to mankind, we end up fighting among ourselves!"

Fantastic though they may be, these superheroes were real people under their jumpsuits, with very human flaws and failings. Reed, their leader, was egotistical and arrogant and could be a bore when describing his latest scientific breakthrough. Sue could be flighty and at times let her emotions get the better of her. Johnny was immature, selfish, and impetuous—all common traits of the average American teenager. Ben was hot-tempered, violent, and full of self-pity for the terrible hand that fate had dealt him. At times, the bickering superheroes more closely resembled a dysfunctional family than an efficient fighting team.

While all four were intriguing characters, it was the Thing who was the real star. His verbal tirades, skillfully written by Lee, ranged from the

The Thing, one of Lee's most vividly written characters, is the only member of the Fantastic Four who cannot transform back into human form.

tragic to the comic. It's the down-to-earth Thing who's forever deflating Reed's overblown language with a wisecrack or trading insults with Johnny. The Fantastic Four were real people in extraordinary situations, and comic book readers immediately embraced them. The very first issue was a sellout, and both Lee and Goodman knew they had something very special on their hands.

The Fantastic Four were unique in other ways, too. While DC's Superman and Batman hid their identities behind alter egos Clark Kent and Bruce Wayne, Reed and his team did not attempt any such disguises. They were who they were and even opened an office in a downtown skyscraper. While they resided in the fictional Central City in their first issue—as make-believe as Superman's Metropolis or Batman's Gotham City—in the second issue, they moved to New York City, home of Stan Lee. New York, with its familiar skyline and high-voltage energy, became the colorful background for nearly every other new superhero the company would create. Most intriguing of all, these various superheroes began running into each other on the streets of Manhattan, something DC heroes rarely did.

Lee decided his company needed a new name to match the originality of its new superheroes. Fondly recalling the original *Marvel Mystery Comics* that first starred Captain America and the Human Torch, he persuaded Goodman to change Atlas's name to Marvel Comics.

A GALLERY OF SUPER VILLAINS

If a superhero is only as good as the villains that he or she struggles against, then the Fantastic Four were blessed with some of the best, or

THE MICRO·WORLD OF **DOCTOR DOOM!**

WITH SPECIAL GUEST STAR: THE AMAZING **ANT-MAN!**

2 PULSE-POUNDING PAGES!!

THE WORLD'S MOST DANGEROUS SUPER-VILLAIN!

SCRIPT: STAN LEE

JACK KIRBY

MEET ANT-MAN IN THIS ISSUE

All of Lee's characters, including his villains, were multi-dimensional.

worst villains ever created. Lee and Kirby came up with bad guys such as the Mole Man, Psycho-Man, the Puppet-Master, and the Impossible Man, an alien who could change his shape at will. Impossible Man proved so popular that he was soon starring in his own comic book.

But the most memorable villain the Fantastic Four ever faced (and they faced him many times) was Doctor Doom. Outfitted in a heavy coat of armor and wearing a steel mask to hide his scarred face, Doctor Doom was the model for *Star Wars'* Darth Vader. Lee and Kirby made him a larger-than-life villain. He wasn't simply a master criminal but the king of the fictional European country of Latveria. His ambition was to conquer the world and run it with the same iron hand as he ran his kingdom. Because of his foreign status, Doom had diplomatic immunity and could not be arrested by the American authorities, a nice touch on Lee's part.

But just as there was some bad in the good guys, there was some good in Doctor Doom. As a brilliant young man, he had attended the same university as Reed Richards and almost became his roommate. But somewhere along the line, Doom's genius went to the dark side.

Another intriguing villain was Sub-Mariner, who was also revived from the Marvel past. A ruler of his own continent, the Lost Land of Atlantis, Sub-Mariner set out to avenge his lost people. At times, he became the Fantastic Four's ally in fighting evil. As the series developed, there were other firsts. Reed and Sue married, becoming the first super-hero couple in comic book history to tie the knot. Soon after, they had their first child, Franklin.

Lee's writing created vivid characters and sparkling dialogue, but Jack Kirby's art was indispensable to making the Fantastic Four fantastic. In the early issues, he didn't tamper with the traditional nine panels per comic book page. But once the title had built up a large audience, he felt secure enough to experiment. Kirby's images exploded on the page. Panels expanded to contain the dynamic energy of the motion-filled figures. Each character was drawn for the maximum dramatic effect in Kirby's inimitable style.

"Marvel's battles had a visceral impact, visually and dramatically, that energized the entire story," wrote Peter Sanderson in *Marvel Universe*. "Lee and Kirby devised brilliant concepts and characterizations that continue to seize readers' imaginations to this day."

ENTER THE HULK

The success of the Fantastic Four changed the face of comic books. For the first time, Stan Lee wasn't following the trends; he was setting them for others to follow. Superheroes were in vogue again after a long absence, and many of the other comic genres—Westerns, romance, sci-fi—all but disappeared from the newsstands. Goodman was anxious to capitalize on their success and told Stan to come up with another superhero team. But again, Stan wanted to try something different—a superhero who was

The isolation exemplified by the Incredible Hulk attracted young readers who could identify with him.

more monster than hero, a character like the Thing, but bigger, stronger, and wilder. Enter the Incredible Hulk, in 1962.

The Incredible Hulk was a kind of modern-day Dr. Jekyll and Mr. Hyde. Like Reed Richards, Bruce Banner—the Hulk's human form—is a brilliant scientist who is exposed to gamma rays while testing a nuclear bomb he has created. (Stan Lee later confessed that he knew next to nothing about science and had no idea what the effects, if any, of cosmic and gamma rays were.) After that, whenever he is threatened or angry, Banner is transformed into a brutish creature, a cross between Frankenstein's monster and a Neanderthal man. Unlike the Thing, who cannot change back to his former self, the Hulk regularly returns to being Banner.

The Hulk, one comic historian has claimed, was "the most unstable character in comics history." And he was also the most alienated. Lacking the support of close friends that the Thing enjoyed, he wandered the deserts and flatlands of the Southwest, seeking solitude but somehow always being drawn into a battle between good and evil. Like the other Marvel superheroes, the Hulk was often misunderstood by the people he was trying to help and protect. They resented, envied, and feared him.

It is this sense of alienation from other people that made Marvel's superheroes so compelling to their young audience. After all, teenagers who read these comics were just as troubled and confused and misunderstood as the Human Torch, the Thing, and the Hulk. In his next creation, Stan Lee would take this concept to its inevitable conclusion and create a superhero who would surpass even Superman himself in popularity.

One of Stan Lee's most famous characters, Spider-Man debuted in the last issue of a discontinued series.

The Marvel Age

Stan Lee loved creating slogans almost as much as he loved creating new superheroes. Marvel's new slogan was "Welcome to the Marvel Age of Comics." Others were soon calling it the Silver Age of Comics, comparing it favorably to the Golden Age of the late 1930s and early 1940s.

The character who made the Silver Age gleam its brightest came to Lee as he watched a fly crawl up his office wall. What if a human had the ability to climbs walls and hang from ceilings? He also recalled fondly a pulp magazine character from his childhood who was called the Spider. There was nothing really spiderish about this masked vigilante, but Lee liked the name.

SPIDER-MAN'S DEBUT

If Stan expected Martin Goodman to be as enthusiastic about his latest brainstorm as he had been about the earlier ones, he was to be sorely disappointed. The publisher thought a superhero who was a spider was a terrible idea. Goodman insisted that people hated spiders. He also didn't like Lee's idea of making this new superhero a teenager. Teens had traditionally been sidekicks and helpmates to superheroes, like Batman's Robin, the Boy Wonder. While the Human Torch was a teenager, he was part of a team and didn't stand alone as a superhero.

Lee was discouraged by Goodman's reaction, but he didn't give up on Spider-Man. When it was announced that Marvel's *Amazing Fantasy* sci-fi comic was about to be discontinued, Lee had an idea. Since nobody much cared what went into the last issue of a failed comic book, he decided to slip in a story about Spider-Man. He brought the character to his favorite collaborator, Jack Kirby. Kirby's concept of Spider-Man's alter ego, Peter Parker, was that of a robust and confident young man. It didn't jibe at all with the scrawny, unassuming teen Lee had imagined.

So he took Spider-Man to Steve Ditko, another gifted Marvel artist. Ditko's rendering of the character was far more thoughtful and stylish. Peter Parker became, as Lee conceived him, a vulnerable fifteen-year-old with little self-confidence.

Amazing Fantasy #15 appeared in September 1962 with Spider-Man on the cover. The issue was a smash. When Martin Goodman saw the sales figures, he was eager for Lee and Ditko to put Spider-Man into his own series, claiming all along that he thought it was a great idea!

Steve Ditko—
Co-Creator of Spider-Man

Jack Kirby brought out the strength and heroic qualities of Marvel superheroes, but Steve Ditko's more subtle style often revealed their fragile humanity. No one captured the vulnerability of Peter Parker and Spider-Man better than Ditko, although he initially drew the character for only the first four years of its long life. According to writer Bradford Wright, "Ditko's own reputation within the field as a reclusive loner and a fierce individualist suggests that the artist put something of himself into the character."

Ditko was born on November 2, 1927, in Johnstown, Pennsylvania. As a young man, he went to New York and studied comic art at the Cartoonists and Illustrators School. He started working as a comic book artist in 1953 and came to Marvel three years later, dividing his time between Marvel and Charlton Comics. When he left Marvel in 1966 over a dispute with Stan Lee, Ditko moved to Charlton Comics full-time. There he worked on and created such lesser-known superheroes as Captain Atom, the Blue Beetle, and the Question. He moved to DC Comics two years later and created the Creeper and the Hawk and Dove. Ditko returned to Marvel in 1979 and drew Spider-Man again for a while beginning in 1988. Now close to eighty years old and still working, Steve Ditko is considered one of the greatest comic book artists of all time.

Peter Parker, Spider-Man's alter ego, began as an awkward and insecure teen. Young readers identified with his internal struggles.

A NEW KIND OF SUPERHERO

What made Spider-Man click instantly with young readers? The answer lies in another Stan Lee slogan that billed Spider-Man as "the hero that could be you." While the Hulk and the Fantastic Four were real human beings, they were nearly all adults. Peter Parker was just a kid like most of his readers, with the same everyday problems and stresses. Adolescents could relate to Spidey, as he became affectionately known at Marvel, because he was one of them—in every way but one.

Spider-Man's origins were revealed in his first appearance. Parker is bitten by a radioactive spider in science class and becomes spiderlike. Not technically a true superhero, he relies on special weapons and devices, many of which he invents himself, such as the webs he shoots out to trap criminals. Also unlike most superheroes, Spider-Man is a reluctant crime fighter. He even fails to help a passing policeman capture a fleeing crook. Later, the same crook shoots and kills his beloved Uncle Ben in a robbery. Haunted by grief and guilt, Parker decides he will face up to his responsibilities and become a crime fighter.

Spider-Man's own comic book first appeared in March 1963. As the series progressed, he was hardly an ordinary superhero. Lee and Ditko devoted almost as much story time to the ordinary day-to-day drama of Parker's life as they did to his battles against super-villains. Readers watched him grow from an insecure teen to a confident young man, who still had his share of problems. He struggled just as mightily with himself as with any mastermind of crime—always questioning, always doubting, always measuring the consequences of his actions.

SPIDEY'S SUPPORTING CAST

Like Clark Kent, Superman's alter ego, Parker got a job with a newspaper. He was a freelance photographer for the *Daily Bugle* and the only photographer who could get pictures of Spider-Man. (No surprise there.) His publisher, J. Jonah Jameson, detested Spider-Man as much as any arch villain did and vowed to expose him, never realizing that all the time Spider-Man was right under his nose.

Peter lived with his elderly Aunt May, whom he faithfully cared for after his uncle's death. His girlfriend was the gorgeous redhead Mary Jane Watson, whom he wooed for years and eventually wed. For the criminal masterminds that Spider-Man battled, Lee and Ditko came up with some of the most ghastly villains in "comicdom". Many had the predatory habits and looks of animals, including the Vulture, the Beetle, the Chameleon, and the Rhino. Then there was the Green Goblin—in reality, industrialist Norman Osborne, the father of Peter's best friend, Harry. When a scientific experiment goes wrong, Osborne is transformed into the gargoylish Goblin, who gradually goes mad and is obsessed with destroying Spider-Man. After the Goblin's demise, Harry Osborne seeks revenge on Spider-Man, never suspecting that his best friend is his father's killer. He eventually assumes his father's identity and calls himself the Hobgoblin.

The ultimate moral problem Spider-Man faced, however, involved Doctor Otto Octavius, better known as Doctor Octopus, or Doc Ock. This mad scientist, with four robotic arms that resemble the tentacles of an octopus, became Spider-Man's number-one nemesis. Doc Ock meets Aunt May and begins a romance with her. How does Parker, whose secret identity neither Doc Ock nor Aunt May suspects, deal with this delicate situation? Just another difficult day in the life of Spider-Man!

Doctor Octopus, a mad scientist, becomes Spider-Man's arch nemesis.

THE MARVEL METHOD

With the success of Spider-Man, Marvel Comics became the biggest comic book company in America, if not the world. Spider-Man—called L'homme-araignée in French and L'uomo regno in Italian—became an international hit.

Just as fans related to the Marvel superheroes on a personal level, Stan Lee saw to it that the fans related to him and his creative team in similar terms. In these comic books, he included a letter page—not a new idea, but his had none of the editorial stuffiness of DC or other companies. It wasn't "Dear Editor" at the top of a fan letter, but "Hi, Stan." He responded with "Hey, Ed" (or whatever the writer's first name was), never "Dear Reader." He also came up with a list of catchphrases that quickly became household words. He'd end an editorial on "Stan's Soapbox" page with "Nuff said" and a letter with the closing "Hang loose."

When competitors began to copy these phrases in their letter columns, Stan was justifiably upset. He finally came up with a word that he didn't think they would copy because they wouldn't know what it meant. The word was *Excelsior!*—a Latin word roughly meaning "upward and onward to greater glory!" It became Stan's signature sign-off and the title of his autobiography.

In his continuing efforts to make readers feel they knew the "Marvel family," Lee gave credit not only to the writers and artists, but also to the people who did the inking and lettering—something never done before in a comic book. Each contributor had a nickname, too. It was Stan (the Man) Lee and Jack (King) Kirby or sometimes "Jolly" Jack Kirby. There was "Sturdy" Steve Ditko and "Jazzy" Johnny Romita. Stan sometimes made the credits even more boisterous: "Invincibly inked by Jovial Joe Sinnott" and "Lethargically lettered by Adorable Artie Simek."

Humor was the hallmark of all Stan Lee's shenanigans, and this endeared him to Marvel fans. On the cover of *The Amazing Spider-Man* #16, he issued the following warning: "If you don't say this is one of the greatest issues you've ever read, we may never talk to you again!" In January 1965, he teased readers with the initials MMMS, which stood for a new fan club, and he challenged readers to guess the club's name. No one guessed that the letters stood for the Merry Marvel Marching Society. Its slogan was: "We don't know where we're marching, but we're on the way!" The thousands of fans who sent in their money to join the MMMS were sent back a membership card, a writing pad, a membership pin, and a memorable record of the Marvel gang having an impromptu gab session. These touches were almost as much of an attraction as the comic books themselves.

GODS AND BILLIONAIRES

Lee and Kirby were literally teeming with new ideas for superheroes. Over the next three years, they developed most of the classic Marvel characters. Spider-Man was followed by a hero who couldn't have been more different from the insecure teenager Peter Parker. Instead of turning to science gone wrong for his next creation, Lee looked to the heavens. His new superhero was a god from Norse mythology. The Mighty Thor, the Norse God of Thunder, made his first appearance in the August 1962 issue of the anthology *Journey into Mystery*. Stan's brother, Larry, now a regular contributor, wrote the story, and the always-reliable

Jack Kirby drew it, noted Lee, "as though he had spent his whole life in Asgard, the home of the gods."

The story of Thor's origin was again tied to a man of science—this time, the sickly physician Don Blake. On a vacation to Norway, Blake is attacked by aliens and hides in a cave, where he discovers Thor's hammer. When he strikes it against a wall, he is transformed into the mighty god. As the series developed, Thor overshadowed his Blake alter ego. Then Blake, in a complicated plot twist, turned out to have been Thor all along. He had been turned into a human by his father, Odin, king of the Norse gods, to break his pride. Loki, the god of mischief and Thor's evil foster brother, became his arch enemy and one of Marvel's most satisfying villains. Lee and

Lee and Kirby based Thor, as well as several other short comics, on Norse mythology.

Lee was inspired by current events, the war in Vietnam, to create Tony Stark, aka Iron Man, a ruthless munitions dealer who transforms into a heroic figure fighting for justice.

Kirby became so absorbed in Norse mythology that they introduced a feature in the comic called *Tales of Asgard* that often featured adaptations of other Norse myths.

From ancient mythology, Lee next turned to the day's headlines. War was brewing in Vietnam, and his next superhero began as Tony Stark, a ruthless billionaire industrialist who invented and sold munitions to the military. Stark was sent to South Vietnam to observe the testing of some of his new weapons when he was captured and seriously wounded by communists. They forced the dying Stark, who had a bullet dangerously close to his heart, to build a new weapon for them. Instead, Stark built a suit of armor for himself with a pacemaker to keep his heart going. In his robotic-looking armor, he was transformed into Iron Man and escaped back to the United States. In an interesting twist on the secret identity theme,

Stark declared that Iron Man was his bodyguard and put him on the company payroll. Literally undergoing a change of heart, Stark became a heroic figure fighting for truth and justice. Created at the height of the Cold War, Iron Man often battled communist foes, such as his Soviet counterpart, the Crimson Dynamo. Soviet premier Nikita Khrushchev even appeared in the comic from time to time.

A STRANGE DOCTOR AND A REVIVED PATRIOT

Probably the strangest superhero to emerge from Lee's imagination was Dr. Strange, Master of the Mystic Arts. Another driven professional, Stephen Strange was a world-renowned surgeon whose hands were irreparably damaged in a car accident. Unable to perform surgery, he sought help from others and ended up on a mountaintop in Tibet, where he became the disciple of a mysterious mystic called the Ancient One. Learning all the secrets of the Ancient One's mystical arts, Strange returned to the United States and settled down in New York's Greenwich Village. From there, he went forth to battle the supernatural forces of evil. Steve Ditko had a field day creating a surreal landscape for Strange and his foes. Dr. Strange quickly became a favorite of the counterculture of the 1960s.

Not all Marvel's superheroes were new. Just as Lee had resurrected the Sub-Mariner and, after a fashion, the Human Torch, now he brought back Captain America, Timely's first and foremost superhero. This simpleminded patriot seemed a strange superhero for the new Marvel, but Lee gave the character a twist that made him fit right in. Frozen in chilly Arctic waters for twenty years following a plane crash near the end of

World War II, Captain America is brought out of suspended animation and dropped into a contemporary world that he finds bewildering. Bucky Barnes, his youthful sidekick, had been killed in the crash, and this motivated Captain America to form the Avengers, a new team of superheroes that originally included the Hulk, the Human Torch, Iron Man, and two lesser-known Marvel creations, Ant Man and the Wasp. As time went on, the team members would change and Captain America would eventually get his own comic book.

BIRTH OF THE X-MEN

Next, Lee wanted to make another team of superheroes, but this time they would all be teenagers. They were not ordinary teens, but mutants, born with strange bodies and extraordinary abilities. He wanted to call

Lee created the first team of superheroes who were the same age as their most avid fans.

them the Mutants, but Martin Goodman insisted that their readers wouldn't know what the word *mutants* meant. So instead, Lee called them the X-Men, after the initial of their mentor, the wheelchair-bound Professor Xavier. The "X" also refers to their "extra" abilities. The original X-Men were the Angel, who had wings for flying; the Iceman, capable of freezing his enemies; Marvel Girl, who had telekinetic powers; Cyclops, whose weapon was powerful rays he emitted from his eyes; and the Beast, a variation on the Hulk.

Like many Marvel characters, the X-Men would change over the years, depending on the writer and artist working on them. After a long slump, the team would emerge in the 1980s as Marvel's most popular superheroes after Spider-Man, with new members such as Wolverine, the most popular X-Man of all.

The last classic Marvel hero to appear in 1964 was Daredevil, who really wasn't a superhero at all. An ordinary man, Matt Murdock was blinded while rescuing a blind man. Although sightless, his other senses were heightened to an incredible degree, and he developed a new radar sense that helped him feel the presence of people and objects. He became a masked vigilante, or crime fighter, called Daredevil. In a bizarre twist, Murdock, who is a lawyer, defended the same criminals he brought to justice as Daredevil!

Marvel had truly become the leader of the comic book industry by the mid-1960s. Just as the company had undergone tremendous change, so were great changes in the works for the man who helped make it all possible—Stan Lee.

Lee (right) was popular with readers, which made him the face of Marvel Comics.

Comic Book Ambassador

arvel's popularity made Stan Lee a hero to millions. Many people saw him as not just the public face of Marvel, but its sole creator. This did not go over well with other creative members of his team, especially key artists Jack Kirby and Steve Ditko.

Bad feelings developed between Lee and the two artists. Lee felt strongly that, as writer, he was the central creator of Marvel's characters. Still, he recognized that both Kirby and Ditko played critical roles in developing the characters and bringing them to life. He even sent Ditko a letter acknowledging him as Spider-Man's co-creator. It may have been too little too late. The two men stopped talking to each other and only communicated through go-betweens. Ditko finally left Marvel in 1966 and was hired by rival DC Comics two years later. At DC, Ditko created Marvel-like heroes such as the Hawk and the Dove, and the Creeper, a superhero capable of changing his shape at will.

CHANGING TIMES

The mid-1960s were a troubled time. The United States was stuck in the highly unpopular Vietnam War (1964-1975), while blacks, Latinos, and women were calling for more civil rights. The country became sharply divided as people took sides for and against the war and other social issues. Marvel and its colleagues in the comic book industry were caught in the middle.

Many people protested the United States' involvement in the Vietnam War. Attempting to avoid controversy, Lee decided to make all Marvel comics completely nonpolitical in 1968.

Traditionally, comic books have seen the world in the black-and-white terms of good versus evil. They were comfortable promoting core patriotic values, as Timely did during World War II. The world had changed considerably since then, however. When the Mighty Thor did battle with the communist Viet Cong forces in Vietnam, this appeared to be an indirect support of the Vietnam War. Many readers responded with less enthusiasm than Marvel expected. This bothered Lee as more and more Americans opposed the conflict. In 1968, he decided to make all Marvel comics completely nonpolitical.

This is not to say that Marvel heroes had no opinions on the state of America. Spider-Man and other superheroes were pro-American in a vague kind of way, opposed not only to crime but also to the conditions of poverty in American cities that often breed it.

A NEW DIVERSITY

When it came to ethnic diversity, Lee and Marvel took a more positive stand in their comics. In 1966, Lee introduced comic books' first African American superhero, the Black Panther. This character had nothing to do with the controversial black militant group of that time called the Black Panthers. He was a prince of a secret African kingdom that was supposedly the most civilized nation on Earth. The Black Panther, who became a figure of African American pride, first appeared in an issue of *The Fantastic Four* and remained their staunch ally for three decades.

A second, more homegrown black superhero was the Falcon, who made his debut in 1969. Like other traditional superheroes, the Falcon led a double life. In the everyday world, he was Sam Wilson, a Harlem social worker who supported civil rights but opposed black separatism.

In 1972, Lee created a third black character, Luke Cage, Hero for Hire. He was modeled after Hollywood heroes such as Shaft and Superfly, stars of the then-popular so-called "blaxploitation" movies. These movies featured black actors in tough, James Bond–type roles. Unlike his Marvel predecessors, Cage was rough, ghetto raised, and street-smart and had his own comic book. Cage was serving time in prison for a crime he didn't commit, when a doctor offered him parole for participating in a scientific experiment. The experiment, as usual, went awry, and Luke gained superhuman powers. He broke out of prison and, in order to make a living, became the first comic book superhero who was a mercenary, or fighter for hire. Luke Cage didn't catch on with readers, and Lee soon transformed him into Power Man, a more run-of-the-mill superhero.

Other minorities got their own superheroes at Marvel. White Tiger (1977) was a Hispanic superhero, a supporting character in Spider-Man's

In Marvel comics, as well as most others, female superheroes were rarely the lead character, nor were they popular with the mostly male readers.

adventures. Red Wolf, a Native American superhero who fought bad guys in the Old West, died a quick death. So did another Native American, Thunderbird, one of the new generation of X-Men. Shang-Chi, a Chinese martial arts hero, was more successful. He first appeared in 1973, and his comic, *Master of Kung Fu*, ran from 1974 to 1983. But Sunfire, a Japanese superhero, was a flop.

A pioneer in developing ethnic characters, Marvel's record with female superheroes was not so impressive. Sue Storm, the Invisible Girl, eventually became the Invisible Woman, but her place in the Fantastic Four was always secondary to the male heroes, and she rarely played a leadership role. Lee attempted to add some new women superheroes to his growing stable in the early 1970s. But characters such as Shanna the She-Devil, a jungle superhero, and the Cat sold poorly and were quickly dumped. The Cat was jointly written and drawn by two women, a rarity in the then male-dominated world of comic books. Not all the blame for these failed female superheroes can be laid on Lee and Marvel. Most readers of action-adventure comics were boys, and they had little interest in female superheroes. DC's popular Wonder Woman was an exception to the rule.

THE SILVER SURFER

If there was one Marvel character who showed that Stan Lee cared about the plight of the modern world in the turbulent 1960s and early 1970s, it was the Silver Surfer. This alien from another planet first appeared in 1966 as a supporting character in an issue of *The Fantastic Four*. He didn't appear in his own comic book until 1968.

Spider-Man, Anti-Drug Crusader

Marvel Comics may not have been in the forefront of social issues in the early 1970s. But the company did take a strong, unapologetic stand on one important issue—drugs. In 1970, the National Institute of Mental Health, a branch of the Department of Health, Education, and Welfare, came to Stan Lee and asked that he put out a series of comic books campaigning against drug abuse. Lee enthusiastically said yes and created an anti-drug Spider-Man issue. When it came before the Comics Code Authority, the group refused to approve the issue. Although the entire story line was against drugs, the fact that drugs were a part of the story at all was against the code's rules. Frustrated by this illogic, Stan went ahead and released the issue anyway, without the CCA's seal of approval on its cover.

The Spider-Man issue was a huge success and received favorable press from many quarters. It was a welcome antidote to years of criticism for comic books as "corrupters of youth." Here was a superhero who was a positive role model to his readers and speaking out against drugs.

Lee's bold stand led to changes in the CCA that allowed publishers to portray adult themes and serious issues in a mature manner in their comic books. Comics were growing up, and Marvel, once again, was leading the way.

The Silver Surfer was considered by comic book connoisseurs as Stan Lee's most serious and sophisticated creation. He came to Earth as a kind of celestial scout for the monstrous planet eater Galactus. After seeing both the strengths and weaknesses of humankind, the Surfer had a change of heart and saved the planet from destruction. He was punished for his bold act by Galactus, who set up a barrier around Earth's atmosphere, making the Silver Surfer a virtual prisoner on the planet. Hated by his own kind and misunderstood by the people of Earth, the Silver Surfer roamed the skies, observing human life as an outsider and doing what he could to save the planet from itself.

The Silver Surfer was a unique figure in the world of comic books. An almost Christlike figure, he reflected and philosophized regularly on the state of the Earth's environment and other problems. Never a big seller, he was wildly popular with intellectuals and college students. The

The Silver Surfer is one of Stan Lee's most serious characters and one of his favorites.

Silver Surfer disappeared after only eighteen issues, although the Surfer character returned in a supporting role in other comics. He remains a favorite among comic enthusiasts and Stan Lee himself.

BIG MAN ON CAMPUS

In the fall of 1968, Martin Goodman sold Marvel Comics to the Perfect Film and Chemical Corporation (later known as Cadence Industries) for about $15 million. The corporation, quite to Lee's surprise, offered him the position of publisher of Marvel Comics. Goodman, who was now president and publisher of the company's new magazine wing, objected. He wanted the Marvel job for his son, who had no experience in comic book publishing. When Lee got the job, Goodman labeled him "disloyal." "By this time I didn't care what Martin said or thought," Lee wrote in his autobiography. "I was finally free to do what I had always felt could and should be done with Marvel, and that was all that mattered."

Lee's plans for Marvel were ambitious. He saw no reason why the comic company couldn't one day be as big a media giant as the Disney company. He set out to make Marvel Comics a household term, and he decided that he himself was Marvel's best salesman. He left the brunt of the writing and creative work to Roy Thomas, who became editor-in-chief, and set out on the road. Lee went to one of Marvel's biggest fan bases—college campuses. Over the next decade and a half, he gave an average of a lecture a week at colleges and universities across the nation. Young people loved Stan's enthusiasm for the comics they had grown up reading. They agreed with him when he said that comics were more than mere entertainment for children and deserved to be a respected part of American popular culture. To show how far the industry had come since Lee first joined it, he was made an adjunct professor of popular culture in 1971 at Bowling Green State University in Bowling Green, Ohio.

The previous year, Stan had established the Academy of Comic Book Art (ACBA), which he hoped would put the comic industry on a level with such other media as film, television, and radio. The ACBA sponsored comic art exhibitions, gave awards to distinguished artists and writers, and promoted comic books in general. Unfortunately, it proved a costly venture with little outside support, and it folded in 1975.

Besides lecturing, Lee turning to writing books about Marvel comics. He put out *Origins of Marvel Comics* in 1974 and *Sons of Origins* in 1975. These books were followed by *Bring on the Bad Guys* (1976), a tribute to Marvel's colorful villains; *The Superhero Women* (1977); and *How to Draw Comics the Marvel Way* (1978).

In the 1970s and early 1980s, Lee lectured in universities across the country about the importance and significance of comic books.

CORPORATE CHANGES AND A COMIC STRIP

In 1972, Martin Goodman left Marvel to form a new comic book company, which he called Atlas, his old company name. A succession of executives filled Goodman's position until business executive Jim Galton took over the reins as president in 1975. Galton respected Lee as the creative head of Marvel and let him do what he wanted, something Stan was very grateful for. The two men shared a good working relationship until Galton left Marvel in 1990.

By 1976, Lee was anxious to expand Marvel into film and television. What he hadn't thought about was turning his superheroes into newspaper comic strip characters. But this is what Denny Allen invited him to do that year. Allen ran a newspaper group called Register and Tribute Syndicate (later to become King Syndicate). Lee opposed the idea from the start. He saw no way that the tight pacing of his comic books could be successfully adapted to the demands of a daily comic strip. But Allen was persistent. He made the offer even more tempting by giving Lee complete artistic control. And the comic strip he wanted was Marvel's biggest star, Spider-Man.

Lee finally gave in, and in January 1977, the first Spider-Man comic appeared in newspapers, with Lee as writer and John Romita as artist. In just one month, Spider-Man was appearing in more than two hundred newspapers. The number eventually grew to five hundred papers worldwide. Lee continues to write the Spider-Man strip for Sunday newspapers, more than thirty years after it started. Lee's brother, Larry Lieber, writes the strips for the daily newspapers. To date, it is the longest-running newspaper comic strip based on a superhero.

John Romita

John Romita was a veteran Marvel artist when he began work on the Spider-Man comic strip with Lee. He had come to Timely Comics in 1949, "ghosting" comic stories for a friend while holding down a job at a lithograph company. (Ghosting is drawing for another artist's comic strip without credit.) He later found out that his friend was working for Stan Lee. "I worked for Stan for six months before he knew I was working for him," he later recalled.

Romita had worked at Timely for eight years when he was let go during severe cutbacks of 1958. He got a job at DC Comics drawing romance stories, which he intensely disliked. Romita returned to Lee and Marvel in 1965 and worked on the superhero Daredevil. Six months later, after Steve Ditko left, Stan asked him to take over drawing Spider-Man. Romita stayed faithful to Ditko's original style for the first few years. Then he began to make the character his own.

"Stan Lee used to come up to me and say I was making him too good-looking," he said in one interview. "I'm making him too brawny. But I couldn't stop myself. It was the only way I could draw him."

Today, most longtime Spider-Man fans are more familiar with Romita's Spider-Man, simply because he drew the character for many more years than Ditko did. In 1972, Romita became Marvel's art director, serving as a mentor and role model for a new generation of Marvel artists. Among them was his son, John Romita Jr., who has since become a respected Marvel artist in his own right.

Marvel's superheroes first appeared on television in cartoons and later in live-action series.

SEVEN

Expanding the Empire

The idea of bringing Marvel characters to television was not a new one in the late 1970s. There had been two attempts to do so a decade earlier. Marvel Superheroes (1966) was a half-hour animated Saturday morning series for children. Each week, it featured one of five Marvel superheroes—Captain America, the Incredible Hulk, Iron Man, Thor, and Sub-Mariner. The show was on a tight budget, and the animation was crude. It disappeared after one season.

A second cartoon series, *The Fantastic Four*, debuted the following year. It was produced for ABC by Hanna-Barbera studios, the biggest name in television cartoon programming. The series ran for three seasons. Then it was resurrected in 1978 on NBC, produced this time by the veteran animation team of David DePatie and Friz Freleng.

The Incredible Hulk, with Lou Ferrigno as the title character, was a surprise hit, and Marvel's first in television.

THE HULK COMES TO TV

Marvel moved away from animation for the first time in 1978 when two of its superheroes were chosen for live-action series on TV. The shows were aired during prime time—the evening hours, when the viewing audience is the largest—which is where Lee believed his characters belonged. A pilot episode of *The Amazing Spider-Man*, starring Neill Hammond as Marvel's most popular superhero, aired on CBS in the fall of 1977. The series next appeared for a five-week run in the spring of 1978. Reaction was lukewarm, however, and the show never ran on a regular basis after that. Stan complained that the plots were aimed at the juvenile market and that TV's Spider-Man, unlike Lee's original creation, was a cardboard hero with little personality.

Much more successful was *The Incredible Hulk*, which debuted on CBS in March 1977 as a mid-season replacement for a canceled show. To everyone's surprise, the show became almost an instant hit and quickly rose to become the number-one show on television.

Most of *The Incredible Hulk's* success was due to Ken Johnson, the writer/director who developed it for Marvel. Johnson had previously worked on the sci-fi series *The Six Million Dollar Man* and *The Bionic Woman*. Unlike earlier Marvel TV directors, Johnson took great liberties with the original characters. He shifted the main focus from the Hulk to his alter ego, Bruce Banner. Bruce, now called David, was played by veteran television actor Bill Bixby.

In the TV series, Banner was a fugitive, hunted by relentless tabloid newspaper reporter Jack McGee, who wanted to expose him to the world as the Hulk. Each episode found Banner wandering from place to place, trying to help people he met in his travels while eluding McGee. Banner's alter ego, the Hulk, was played by former wrestler and bodybuilder Lou Ferrigno. At 6 feet 5 inches and nearly 300 pounds, he fit the part perfectly. Wisely, Johnson limited the Hulk to two short appearances in most episodes, giving his rampages the ultimate dramatic impact. Unlike the comic book character, the Hulk never spoke. This prevented any unintentional humor that would have resulted from the character's fractured comic book English.

With solid scripts and strong direction, *The Incredible Hulk* remained on the air for four full seasons, ending its run in 1982. Stan Lee, who had moved with his wife to Los Angeles in 1980 to oversee Marvel's movie and television production, couldn't have been more pleased.

The Incredible Bill Bixby

When Bill Bixby's agent first approached the actor with the script of *The Incredible Hulk* and said he thought it would interest him, the actor's response was, "You've got to be kidding!" But after he read the script, he felt differently. "The Hulk is the personification of the enemy which lurks under the surface of us all," he said in one interview. "We have to control that enemy within ourselves, or we can't control the condition of the world."

When he took the role of David Banner, Bixby was no newcomer to fantasy TV. In the 1960s, he had starred in *My Favorite Martian* (1964–1966). This was a popular sitcom about a Martian who crash-lands on Earth and moves in with Bixby, who plays a reporter for a Los Angeles newspaper. Bixby also starred in *The Magician*, a short-lived series in 1973 about a nightclub magician who uses magic to solve real-life crimes. Coached by a real magician, the actor performed his own tricks on the show.

After *The Incredible Hulk* folded, the characters returned in three made-for-television movies, all directed and produced by Bixby, who again played David Banner. Three years after the last movie, *The Death of the Incredible Hulk* (1990), Bill Bixby, a hero in his own right, died after a long and valiant battle with prostate cancer.

ROCK GROUPS, TOYS, AND COLLECTIBLES

While the Hulk was making it big on the small screen, Stan Lee was busy getting the rights to do a comic book version of one of the biggest box-office hits of 1977—George Lucas's sci-fi epic *Star Wars*. It seemed perfect for comic books, and Marvel came out with a six-issue comics series based on the movie. It sold more than a million copies. Marvel had similar success adapting the glitter-rock group Kiss into a comics series in 1977. Marvel also did comics based on other rock groups such as the Beatles and the Rolling Stones.

Marvel was outselling DC with its comics throughout the 1970s. But there was one area where Marvel lagged behind its closest rival—licensed products. These are toys and other products featuring a well-known character. To change that, Lee worked out a

Lee had a knack for knowing what would be well suited to the comic book medium, such as the rock group Kiss, which he adapted into a comic series in 1977.

licensing deal with the Mego Toy Company to put out a line of Marvel action figures and play sets.

Marvel was also finding a new way to sell its comics. The old newspaper stores were disappearing, and so were many of the shops where comic books were traditionally sold. Meanwhile, new stores devoted to

By the late 1970s, comic books were becoming a respected, and collected, part of pop culture.

selling comics were cropping up across the country. These new stores bought their comics directly from Marvel. This eliminated the middlemen, the distributors, who cut into the company's profits. From 1976 to 1979, Marvel's sales directly to stores soared from $1.5 million to $3.5 million. Lee's campaign to make comic books a respected part of American pop culture was succeeding. People had begun to collect old comics for fun and investment. Marvel was able to sell its old, leftover issues to collectors at a profit.

But as the Marvel empire expanded, new problems arose. Some people in the industry criticized Lee for focusing on marketing his existing characters instead of creating new and fresh ones. As Marvel lost some of its edge, artists and writers began to defect. They went to DC or to new, independent companies such as First Comics and Eclipse Comics, the first publisher to produce its own trading cards.

A NEW BEGINNING

In 1986, Marvel celebrated its twenty-fifth anniversary. In that quarter century, Marvel and Lee had changed the face of comic books. They had taken a form of entertainment that was once looked down on and made it into a respected art form. The same year, Cadence sold Marvel to New World Enterprises for $50 million. New World was very interested in creating new television series and movies based on the Marvel characters. Stan moved to New World's headquarters in Westwood, California, and looked forward to a new and exciting era in his career. But the success he had enjoyed for so many years was about to face some serious setbacks.

In the late 1980s and early 1990s, Ron Perelman expanded Marvel's merchandising, began developing films based on Marvel characters, and took the business public, listing the company on the New York Stock Exchange.

EIGHT

Not So Marvelous

In 1988, Ron Perelman, the owner of a large group of companies, took over New World Enterprises and Marvel Comics. Perelman had big plans for Marvel, and Stan Lee couldn't have been happier. Lee's salary was tripled, and he was made head of Marvel Films, a new company that would develop films based on Marvel characters.

Perelman formed a partnership with Toy Biz, Inc., to license Marvel toys, including the popular Marvel superhero action figures. About the same time, he bought Fleer, the company that made Dubble Bubble gum. The gum came with baseball trading cards, which had been a big business since the 1950s. In the summer of 1991, Marvel Entertainment, as it was now

The price of Marvel stock fell during the early 1990s, and this left the company vulnerable to a takeover.

called, became the first comic book publisher to be listed on the New York Stock Exchange. That meant the public could buy shares in the company.

THE BUBBLE BURSTS

Then just as it appeared that nothing could go wrong with Marvel, everything did. It started with the company's bread and butter—its comic books. For years, the prices that collectors paid for comics had been spiraling upward. But like many other collectible crazes, this one became increasingly unstable. The prices of back issues climbed so high that even the most avid collectors could no longer afford them. Once people stopped buying collectible comics, prices collapsed. Comic book collections once thought to be worth thousands of dollars were now worth only a fraction of that. As business fell off, comic book stores across

Dark Horse Comics

Dark Horse Comics was founded in 1986 by Mike Richardson in Milwaukie, Oregon. A dark horse, in the horse-racing world, is a little-known horse that makes an unexpectedly good showing. And Dark Horse Comics was exactly that—a dark horse in the competitive world of comic books. With a darker, more contemporary tone, Dark Horse became, in a short time, the third-largest publisher of comics in America, right behind Marvel and DC.

Dark Horse's most popular titles, such as *Hellboy* by Mike Mignola and *Sin City* by Frank Miller, used stories that continued through a dozen or more issues. Both have also been collected into popular graphic novels—fictional stories presented in comic-strip format—and made into movies. Hellboy's gloomy imagery and red-skinned demon character were heavily influenced by the supernatural tales of Edgar Allan Poe and the dynamic drawings of Jack Kirby. *Sin City* shows the influence of 1940s Hollywood film noir, a style of movie filled with dark shadows and dark doings. However, Hellboy's brutal, graphic violence and corrupt, sometimes psychologically deranged characters are disturbingly contemporary.

Dark Horse has featured movie characters (Alien and Indiana Jones) and television characters (Buffy the Vampire Slayer) in their comics. Adding insult to injury, Dark Horse has also put out a line of *Star Wars* comics, a license that once belonged to Marvel.

the country went out of business. In a short time, the number of American comic book specialty stores shrank from 6,000 to 2,000.

Sales of comics in general fell off drastically. In 1993, total sales in the comic book industry came to about $1 billion. Three years later, that figure had fallen by more than half, to $450 million. As if that weren't bad enough, Marvel suddenly found that new rival publishers were luring readers away with their bold, new, edgy comics and superheroes. The most prominent of these rivals were the small, independent companies Dark Horse and Image Comics. Marvel's share of the comic book market—its portion of all comic books sold—shrank from a high of 70 percent in the early 1980s to less than 50 percent by 1999.

Another bad break hurt Marvel's line of baseball trading cards. In 1994, America's professional baseball teams went on strike against their owners. For the first time in memory, there was no professional baseball season in the United States. Interest in buying and trading baseball cards fell off sharply, and sales plummeted.

To stay in business, Marvel and other comics companies tightened their belts and cut costs. That meant firing many talented writers and artists, who went to other companies with lower expenses, such as Dark Horse and Image Comics.

A STRUGGLE FOR CONTROL

Financially weakened by these changes in the marketplace, Marvel became a target for corporate raiders. (A corporate raid is the takeover of a company that doesn't want to be bought. The raider buys the company and sells it for a profit, and the company virtually disappears.) Billionaire investor Carl Icahn wanted to take over Marvel, but Ron Perelman wouldn't give up his company without a fight. In 1996, he took the desperate measure of filing for bankruptcy. This is a company's legal declaration that it is unable to pay its debts. Perelman hoped the negative effects of bankruptcy would keep Icahn away long enough for him to reorganize Marvel and keep it afloat financially. But Icahn was just as determined. He won a ruling in federal court allowing him to take over the company in May 1997.

After a court ruled in his favor, billionaire Carl Icahn took over Marvel in 1997 to the disappointment of Lee and Perelman.

Once in power, Icahn himself reorganized the company. He offered Stan Lee a two-year contract, which he rejected. In a legal fight, Stan regained the lifetime agreement he had previously had with Marvel and was given the title "chairman emeritus." Like a professor emeritus, Stan had all the honors but little meaningful work to do.

Stan continued to write the *Spider-Man* newspaper comic strip and occasionally wrote stories for Marvel comic books. His film projects had

Dolph Lundgren starred as the title character in the 1989 film *The Punisher*.

still met with little success. Two films—*The Punisher* (1989) and *Captain America* (1991)—had both been bombs. They were issued in video form without a major release in theaters. Matt Salinger, the son of writer J. D. Salinger, had played Captain America in the film version. The Punisher, a lone crime fighter who lived in the city sewers, was played by action star Dolph Lundgren.

The Punisher was typical of the new breed of comic heroes of the 1980s. This was a time when the fear of crime in urban centers was growing, and America was seen as a more dangerous place than ever before. The Punisher's story line reflected this mood. Its hero was a former Marine who had served in Vietnam, Frank Castle (later changed to Castiglione). He and his family witnessed a mob hit and were in turn shot by the gangsters. Castiglione alone survived and vowed vengeance. He turned himself into the Punisher, a vigilante waging a deadly, one-man war on crime. This type of hero was a far cry from the human and thoughtful Spider-Man or the Fantastic Four. The magic, and the fun, seemed to have gone out of comic book superheroes.

Nevertheless, Lee still believed in his classic heroes. He continued to pin his highest hopes for a blockbuster movie on Spider-Man. The project, unfortunately, was delayed year after year. It was beginning to look as if a Spider-Man movie might never be made.

STAN LEE MEDIA

After decades of hard work creating comics and promoting them, Lee found himself with little to do. His contract allowed him to pursue his own projects, and he felt ready for a new challenge. Peter F. Paul, the producer of the Spirit of America Awards, honored Lee at the 1991 awards banquet in Beverly Hills, California. Stan was in good company: among the other honorees was former President Ronald Reagan.

Lee ventured into high-tech media—video games and the Internet—with the creation of Stan Lee Media in 1998.

Soon after, Paul approached Stan with an attractive offer. He wanted to form a company with Stan that would take comics into the up-and-coming world of the Internet. Video games and the Internet had made it possible for kids to become their own superheroes by acting out their parts in on-screen games. Next to such high-tech media, comic books looked hopelessly out of date.

Stan was eager to move into this new world and become a player. He accepted Paul's offer. Stan Lee Media was formed in 1998, with Stan as creative head of the company and Paul in charge of the financing. Young, talented writers and artists were hired to work with Stan on a gallery of new characters. Their comics were put on the Web in what they called webisodes. For Stan, it was like starting all over again—but this time, he was making comics the way he wanted to. Before long, Stan Lee Media had 140 employees and a total worth of about $90 million. And then the axe fell.

Unbeknownst to Stan, Paul had been making millions of dollars by illegally buying and selling Stan Lee Media stock. By the end of 2000, the company was out of business. Paul and three associates were charged with illegal trading, and Paul and his family fled to Brazil. He was later arrested there and imprisoned. Stan was in a state of shock. His trusted partner had used him and the company to enrich himself. While Stan was absolved of any involvement in the scandal, it was a blow to his reputation and his career. "I'll never be so stupidly trusting again," he wrote in his autobiography.

But there were better days ahead for Stan Lee and Marvel Comics.

After a more than fifteen-year saga, the first Spider-Man movie was released in 2002 to critical acclaim.

NINE

Spidey Forever

The year 2000 might have been a dark year for Stan Lee, but a glint of sunshine broke through the gloom. After years of negotiations, false starts, and lawsuits, it looked like *Spider-Man*, the movie, was finally going to be made. The rights had gone to Columbia Pictures, and the film was in preproduction.

A MOVIE'S EVOLUTION

The saga of the Spider-Man movie had begun in 1975, when producer Menahem Golan of Cannon Films bought a five-year option on *Spider-Man*. That means he bought the rights to make the film, but he had to do it within five years. In 1990, Golan sold the option to the Carolco film company. Carolco hired director James Cameron, maker of the two *Terminator* movies and *Aliens*, to write a script and direct. This was good news for Stan Lee. He respected Cameron and felt that he was the kind of filmmaker who could do justice to his characters.

Cameron finished a treatment, an outline of the film script, by 1993, at which point things got sticky. Golan decided he wanted control over the Spider-Man movie after all and sued Carolco to get the rights back. Carolco responded by suing Golan in 1994. Then Marvel jumped in and sued both of them to get back the Spider-Man movie rights. A final settlement was reached in 1999, paving the way for Columbia Pictures to make the film. In the Columbia deal, Sam Raimi would be the director. He had already made a successful film about a comic book superhero, Darkman, back in 1990. Stan had worked with Raimi years earlier on a film version of Thor, but the film, *The Mighty Thor*, was never produced. Stan had great confidence in Raimi who Stan believed looked a lot like Peter Parker.

JUST IMAGINE . . .

With *Spider-Man* in production, Stan received perhaps the strangest job offer of his career. In 2000, DC Comics, Marvel's longtime rival, asked him to write a dozen new comic books. The characters would not be new ones created by Lee, but the most respected superheroes in the DC stable—Superman, Batman, and Wonder Woman. For DC, this was a clever way to revive these old, traditional superheroes and draw in new readers.

Stan agreed to the deal, and the series carried the title *Just Imagine Stan Lee's* (name of DC superhero here). All twelve books in the series were sellouts, reflecting well on both the durability of DC's characters and Stan Lee's ability to reinvent them.

Around the same time, another of Stan's "children," the X-Men, hit the screen in a major motion picture. *X-Men* (2000), directed by Bryan Singer, had a big budget and an all-star cast. It featured Patrick Stewart as Professor Charles Xavier, mentor of the mutant superhero group; Hugh Jackman as Wolverine, the new, reluctant member of the team; and Oscar-winner Halle Berry as Storm, a mutant who could whip up storms on demand. British actor Ian McKellen played the villainous Magneto, who wants to create a world of mutants under his control.

X-Men was a huge box-office hit and spawned a sequel, *X-2* (2002). The sequel featured most of the original cast and a new villain, a mutant-hating scientist played by Brian Cox. While *X-2* did well, many critics felt it relied more on special effects and action scenes than on character development, which had made the first film memorable.

TWO BLOCKBUSTERS

Spider-Man was completed at last and released to theaters in the summer of 2002. It starred Tobey Maguire, a rising young actor, as Peter Parker and Spider-Man. Kirsten Dunst played his true love, Mary Jane Watson. Willem Dafoe, a top character actor, turned in a chilling portrayal as the tortured industrialist Norman Osborne, who is transformed into the Green Goblin, Spider-Man's nemesis.

Spider-Man was the summer's biggest box-office success. It reached the $100 million mark in ticket sales in just three days, faster than any other movie to date. It also scored the highest box-office income in a

Tobey Maguire—
Big Screen Spider-Man

The actor who has portrayed Spider-Man in three hit movies faced nearly as many challenges growing up as Peter Parker did. Tobey Maguire was born on June 27, 1975, to unwed parents. His father was a twenty-year-old cook and his mother an eighteen-year-old secretary. When he was two, they split up.

Tobey moved from place to place with his mother, never staying in one location for very long. His first ambition was to become a cook like his father, but his mother offered him $100 if he would take a high school drama class instead of home economics. Tobey took the money and never regretted it. He quit high school and began making the rounds of auditions for child actors. After landing a few commercials and bit parts on television, he was offered a starring role in a sitcom, *Great Scott*. Unfortunately, the show was canceled after only nine weeks.

Maguire began to get parts in movies, playing sensitive, appealing young men. He got critical raves for roles in such major films as The *Cider House Rules* (1999) and *Wonder Boys* (2000). He was not the first choice to play the title role in *Spider-Man*. Among the many other actors who auditioned was his good friend Leonardo DiCaprio. When Maguire auditioned for the part, he had never read a *Spider-Man* comic, but he was deeply impressed by the movie's script. After getting the role, he strenuously trained and dieted for five months to look like a superhero. But it was Maguire's vulnerability and sensitivity in the role that made his Parker/Spider-Man truly memorable.

Spider-Man made Maguire famous and rich. His salary for *Spider-Man* was $4 million. When he made *Spider-Man 2*, his salary shot up to $17 million. Much like Peter Parker, the poor boy from the wrong side of the tracks had traveled far from his beginnings.

single day—$43.6 million, as noted in the *Guinness Book of World Records*. The film was nominated for Academy Awards for Best Sound and Best Visual Effects.

Spider-Man was a great success with movie critics, too. They hailed it as one of that rare breed of summer action-adventure movies that is made with care and intelligence. While the movie was filled with plenty of special effects, they never overwhelmed the characters or the story line. Stan Lee, who served as executive producer, was overjoyed. After

Tobey Maguire brought great sensitivity to the role of Spider-Man, a quality essential to Lee's original character.

years of frustration, he had finally seen his characters brought to the screen the way he wanted them to be. "People have been saying to me for years, 'Why isn't *Spider-Man* a feature film?'" Stan said in one interview. "Now I don't have to answer them anymore." Best of all, Stan—a ham at heart—got a small cameo role in the film, appearing in the scene where the Green Goblin attacks the World Unity Festival.

A *Spider-Man* sequel was planned immediately. Meanwhile, other Marvel characters did not fare as well on the big screen. *Daredevil* and *Hulk*, both released in 2003, fizzled at the box office and were panned by critics and audiences alike. Despite the presence of talented filmmaker Ang

In *Spider-Man 2*, Alfred Molina plays Spider-Man's arch nemesis, Doctor Octopus.

Lee, who directed *Hulk*, and the romantic teaming of Ben Affleck and Jennifer Garner in *Daredevil* (the couple has since married), neither film measured up to the original Marvel comics they were based on.

Fortunately, *Spider-Man 2* (2004) was a different story. If anything, the sequel was better than the first film. Director Raimi was back, along with Maguire and Dunst. Actor Alfred Molina gave a spectacular performance as Doctor Octopus, the great scientist who turned into a multi-limbed evil mastermind. The budget for the film was bigger this time, and the special effects were better. The script, written mostly by Oscar-winning screenwriter Alvin Sargent, deepened the characters and their conflicts. A number of critics called *Spider-Man 2* "the best super-hero movie ever."

Spider-Man 2 was nominated for three Oscars and won one for Best Visual Effects. Together, the first two *Spider-Man* films grossed $1.5 billion in ticket sales worldwide.

STAN BACK IN BUSINESS

While his characters were coming to life for millions of moviegoers, Stan Lee was finding new life for himself in another new venture at the age of eighty. With his lawyer Arthur Lieberman and longtime friend Gill Champion, Lee started a media and entertainment company, Purveyors of Wonders (better known as POW!) Entertainment, in November 2002.

Lee had learned his lesson from the Stan Lee Media disaster. He started POW! modestly, with a small staff. The company's goal was to create and produce live and animated movies, television series, video games, DVDs, and merchandise based on old and new Marvel characters.

The first POW! production to see the light of day was *Stripperella*. This animated television series debuted on Spike TV in June 2003. If the title sounds a little racy for comic book fans, it was meant to be. For Lee, the series was a spoof on his many superhero adventure stories of the past.

The title character was modeled after television actress Pamela Anderson, who also did the voice for Stripperella. She worked as a stripper, but this was just a disguise for her real job as a crime fighter. Everything about *Stripperella* was meant to poke fun at Marvel and other comic book heroes, from the dialogue to the visual gags. The villains included such kooky characters as Cheapo, who specializes in low-budget crimes, and the Bridesmaid, who kidnaps men in her search for the perfect husband. The series was discontinued in 2005.

In January of that year, POW! entered into an agreement with Vidiator Technology to create live-action animation for mobile devices and other wireless media. To date, POW! Entertainment has about forty projects in various stages of development.

Now in his eighties, Stan Lee is still filled with the energy and confidence of youth. He continues to meet his young fans and inspire them with his life and his characters. His autobiography, *Excelsior! The Amazing Life of Stan Lee*, was published in 2002. Stan's novel, *The Alien Factor*, has been considered for the movies, while the much-anticipated *Spider-Man 3*, with the same creative team, is scheduled for release in 2007. Movies based on Iron Man and a brand-new Lee superhero called Foreverman are in the works, too.

"Lee," writes journalist Frank Houston, "is a modern myth-maker. Unlike [*Lord of the Rings* author J. R. R.] Tolkien, his mythology exists in an imagined present. Unlike [*Star Wars* creator George] Lucas, his characters are deep and existential. Lee's vision is at least as humanistic as it is magical."

But the last word comes from Stan Lee himself. "I'm doing just what I've always loved to do, creating characters and concepts with which to entertain the public, but now I'm doing it on the largest playing field of all," he writes at the conclusion of his autobiography. "It's all so different from the first time I started working in comics, when I figured I'd hang with it for a while until I got some experience and then I'd go out and get into the real world. I think I just might be ready now."

Timeline

STAN LEE'S LIFE   WORLD EVENTS

1922 Stanley Martin Lieber is born in New York City, New York, on December 28.

1929 The Stock Market crashes and the Great Depression begins.

1934 The first newsstand comic book, Famous Funnies, is published.

1937 Stan wins an essay contest run by the New York Herald-Tribune.

1940 Stan is hired as a "gofer" at Timely Comics.

1941 Joe Simon and Jack Kirby leave Timely Comics, and Lee is made "temporary" editor and art director.

The United States enters World War II after the bombing of Pearl Harbor by the Japanese on December 7.

1942 Stan enlists in the Army in November and writes training films and manuals during the war.

1945 Stan returns to Timely Comics as editorial and art director.

World War II ends.

1947 Stan marries Joanie Clayton Boocock on December 5.

1950 Stan and Joanie have a daughter, Joan Celia. EC Comics launches its famous horror comics, *The Vault of Horror* and *The Crypt of Terror* (later renamed *Tales from the Crypt*).

1950–1953 The United States is involved in the Korean War.

1954 The Comics Code Authority (CCA) is formed by comic book publishers to fend off attacks on comic book violence and sex.

1958 Artist Jack Kirby returns to Timely Comics, now called Atlas Comics.

1961 The first issue of *The Fantastic Four* is published in November; Atlas changes its name to Marvel Comics.

1962 *The Incredible Hulk* debuts; Spider-Man makes his first appearance in the last issue of *Amazing Fantasy* in September.

1963 *The Avengers* and *The X-Men* make their comic book debut; Spider-Man first appears in his own comic book.

1964 Captain America returns to Marvel Comics in *The Avengers* after nearly a twenty-year absence.

1964–1973 The United States is involved in the Vietnam War.

1966 Steve Ditko, co-creator of Spider-Man, leaves Marvel; Marvel's first black superhero, the Black Panther, appears; the Silver Surfer first appears in a Marvel comic.

1968 Marvel is bought by Perfect Film and Chemical Corporation; Stan becomes Marvel's publisher.

1969 Astronaut Neil Armstrong becomes the first human to walk on the Moon on July 20.

1970 Stan founds the short-lived Academy of Comic Book Art (ACBA); Jack Kirby leaves Marvel.

1974 The Punisher makes his first appearance in *Spider-Man* and Wolverine in *The Incredible Hulk*.

President Nixon resigns in the midst of the Watergate scandal; Vice President Gerald Ford becomes president.

1977 *The Spider-Man* comic strip written by Stan first appears in newspapers in January; Marvel adapts the movie *Star Wars* to comic book form.

1978 *The Incredible Hulk* television series begins its first full season on CBS.

1980 Stan and Joanie move to Los Angeles.

Ronald Reagan is elected president of the United States in November.

1986 New World Enterprises buys Marvel for $50 million; Dark Horse Comics, a Marvel competitor, is founded.

1989 Germany's Berlin Wall is torn down; Eastern Europe is freed from communist rule.

1991 Marvel Entertainment becomes the first comic book publisher to be listed on the New York Stock Exchange.

U.S. and allied troops fight the Persian Gulf War in Iraq.

The Soviet Union breaks up into several separate states.

1994 Artist Jack Kirby dies; the comic book industry begins to experience serious setbacks for a multitude of reasons.

1996 Marvel files for bankruptcy to fend off a corporate takeover.

1998 Lee and partner Peter F. Paul establish Stan Lee Media.

2000 Stan Lee Media folds amidst a financial scandal; the *X-Men* movie premieres.

2001 On September 11, terrorists hijack U.S. airplanes and crash them into the World Trade Center in New York City and the Pentagon in Arlington, Virginia.

2002 *Spider-Man*, the movie, opens in the summer and is a huge hit; Stan establishes a new company, POW! Entertainment, in November; Stan publishes his autobiography.

2003 *Stripperella*, Lee's spoof of superheroes, debuts in June on Spike TV; three Marvel films— *Daredevil, Hulk*, and a sequel to *X-Men*—are released.

U.S. troops and their allies invade Iraq.

2004 *Spider-Man 2* is hailed by critics as "the best superhero movie ever."

2007 *Spider-Man 3* is scheduled for release.

THE CLASSIC MARVEL SUPERHEROES

Superheroes	Superpowers	Major Villains	First Appearance
Captain America	Superhuman strength from experimental serum developed by the military	The Red Skull	Originally in 1941 in *Captain America* Comics; reintroduced in 1964 in *The Avengers*, #4
Dr. Strange (Stephen Strange)	Powers of magic taught him by the Ancient One in Tibet	Nightmare, the Dread Dormammu	1965 in *Strange Tales*, #110
The Fantastic Four (Mr. Fantastic, the Invisible Woman, the Human Torch, the Thing)	Mr. Fantastic can stretch his body in any shape; Invisible Woman can become invisible; Human Torch can turn into flames and fly; the Thing has superhuman strength	Doctor Doom, the Sub-Mariner	1961 in their own comic
The Incredible Hulk (Bruce Banner)	Superhuman strength	Absorbing Man, the Leader, Modok	1962 in his own comic
Iron Man (Tony Stark)	No superpowers; wears a suit of iron that gives him great strength and protection	The Crimson Dynamo	1962 in *Tales of Suspense*, #39

Superheroes	Superpowers	Major Villains	First Appearance
The Mighty Thor	A god with supernatural powers and a magic hammer that helps him fly	Loki, Norse god and Thor's evil foster brother	1962 in *Journey into Mystery*, #83
The Punisher	No superpowers, excellent combat skills	All criminals	1974 in *Spider-Man*, #129
Spider-Man (Peter Parker)	Can climb walls and ceilings like a spider; creates web spinners to shoot out webbing to catch enemies and protect victims	The Green Goblin, the Hobgoblin, Doc Ock	1962 in *Amazing Fantasy*, #15
Wolverine (James Howlett)	Accelerated healing, razor-sharp claws, keen senses	Sabretooth, Magneto	1974 in *The Incredible Hulk*, #180

To Find Out More

BOOKS

Crawford, Hubert H. *Crawford's Encyclopedia of Comic Books*. Middle Village, N.Y.: Jonathan David Publishers, 1978.

Lee, Stan, and George Mair. *Excelsior! The Amazing Life of Stan Lee*. New York: Simon & Schuster, 2002.

Lee, Stan, Jack Kirby, John Romita, and Steve Ditko. *Marvel Visionary: Stan Lee*. New York: Marvel Comics, 2005.

Sanderson, Peter. *Marvel Universe*. New York: Harry N. Abrams, 1996.

Wright, Bradford W. *Comic Book Nation: The Transformation of Youth Culture in America*. Baltimore: The Johns Hopkins University Press, 2001.

DVDS

The Incredible Hulk—The Television Series Ultimate Collection (1978). MCA Home Video, (6 discs), 2003.

Spider-Man (2002). Sony Pictures, 2002.

Spider-Man 2 (2004). Sony Pictures, 2004.

Stan Lee's Mutants, Monsters and Marvels. Sony Pictures, 2002.

X-Men (2000). Twentieth Century Fox, 2001.

ORGANIZATIONS AND ONLINE SITES

Don Markstein's Toonopedia
http://www.toonopedia.com/

Writer Don Markstein calls this site "A Vast Repository of Toonological Knowledge," and that is no exaggeration. It is an exhaustive and always entertaining encyclopedic collection, with more than a thousand entries on not only comic book characters and comic book companies, but also newspaper and magazine comics and movie and television animated cartoons.

Jack Kirby Museum and Research Center
http://kirbymuseum.org/

This highly informative educational site includes complete full-color comic stories from Kirby's archives.

Marvel Comics Official Web Site
http://www.marvel.com/

This heavily commercial site is more for promotional purposes than for dispersing information. It does have some general information about Marvel Comics today and updates on comic books, movies, and merchandising tie-ins.

Stan Lee's Official Web Site
http://www.StanLeeWeb.com/

This attractive site contains a lengthy biography of Stan Lee and a useful timeline, along with news of Stan's many projects and enterprises.

SuperHero Universe
http://www.superherouniverse.com/

This is another heavily commercial site. Once you get past all the products for sale, there are some interesting articles such as "Ronald Reagan and Comic Super Heroes in the '80s." There are also neat statistic sheets on the major Marvel and DC superheroes.

A Note on Sources

A good place to start learning more about Stan Lee is his autobiography, *Excelsior! The Amazing Life of Stan Lee*, co-written with George Mair. It alternates between Stan's voice and Mair's, which fills in the background details. While it's a good read, Stan leaves out many details about his rise to comic fame, and the chronology is at times fuzzy. Interviews and articles about him in periodicals and online fill in many of the gaps.

For the Marvel superheroes that Stan created, *Marvel Universe* by Peter Sanderson is probably the best single volume. Exhaustively researched and lavishly illustrated, it details the histories of most of the best-known Marvel characters from the debut of The Fantastic Four in 1961 to the mid-1990s, when it was published. *Marvel Visionary: Stan Lee* contains some of the best of the classic comic book stories written by Lee and his three best-known collaborators—Jack Kirby, Steve Ditko, and John Romita.

There are a few good books that offer critical analysis of Marvel and other comic books and put them in the context of American culture over the past seventy years. One of the best is *Comic Book Nation: The Transformation of Youth Culture in America* by Bradford Wright.

Index

About the Author

Steven Otfinoski has written more than 120 books for young adults and children. He has written numerous biographies about presidents, explorers, writers, and scientists. He has also written books about countries, states, history, and public speaking. He is the author of *Bram Stoker: The Man Who Wrote Dracula* in the *Great Life Stories* series and *Extraordinary Short Story Writing* in the *Franklin Watts Prep* series. For adults, he has published two books on rock music.

Otfinoski lives in Connecticut with his wife, Beverly, a teacher and editor, and their two children, Daniel and Martha. When he's not writing, he enjoys swimming, tennis, watching movies on DVD, listening to and collecting all kinds of music, and reading nonfiction.